TOFU
INK
ARTS
PRESS

Volume 4

Tofu Ink Arts Press Volume 4
Copyright © 2022 by Brian L. Jacobs, Pasadena, California, USA.
Published by Tofu Ink Arts Press. All rights reserved.
Book design by JLTY Atelier, Singapore.
Cover image: Abstract Borderland 41, courtesy of Octavio Quintanilla.

ISBN: 978-1-958661-00-0

www.TOFUINK.com
A member of CLMP

Dedicated to
Clifton Snider, Neal Climenhaga,
Peter Lamborn Wilson/Hakim Bey and
The People of Ukraine.

"To consecrate the union between elsewhere and possibility,
the poet demanded of himself permanent abstinence
from something impossible."

- Poetics of Relation, Edouard Glissant

CONTENTS

PREFACE

Tofu Ink Arts Press is very excited about the possibilities our poets and artists share in their fabulous work for our *Volume 4* edition. Our writers and artists rupture, mapping at times a-linearly & all proliferating, without boundaries or centers, in the margins without limits, rejecting principles of hegemony, creating a desire, that is always in flux, along new pathways of experimentation.

Tofu Ink contributors manifest possibility; a sort of, what I like to call a **Rhizomatic Poetic.** This poetic inquiry explores diverse artistic acts; poetic discursive narratives, mutating through exploring memory, decolonizing, otherness, romanticization of the other and elicit performances of queer identity with overlapping Rhizomatic voices in errantry. These artists are the true auditors of our world, for discovering every possible elsewhere; a liberating vehicle into possibilities. The arts may be the only medium to weave these difficult tasks.

Tofu Ink Arts Press has come a long way in the year and a half since we have been birthed. Our first issue in Spring 2021 was strictly digital moving into a format for our Summer 2021 issue as an actual journal that we eventually created as an E Reader. Our first print issue was for the beginning of 2022 and exhibited stunning pieces that we were able to exhibit at the March, 2022 AWP conference in Philadelphia, Pennsylvania with a tremendously positive response.

Tofu Ink Arts Press is now venturing into new possibilities by printing single author and artist books for release this year. We have ten books we are currently working on that will be sold online and in books stores worldwide. We will also see you in Seattle for AWP 2023, with a reading panel and booth at the book fair. We are also excited about announcing in November 2022 our *Poetry Prize in honor of Theatre Visionary Reza Abdoh* and our new Arts, plus Chapbook contests.

I would like to acknowledge my amazing EYES, Jojo for his selfless efforts in editing and digital magic. I would also like to thank my husband Michael for listening to my ideas and being patient with me as I create.

Please enjoy this 2022 Summer's selection of Tofu Ink Arts Press.

May 2022

Abol Bahadori Bliss

Abol Bahadori Liberation

Abol Bahadori Fallings

Abol Bahadori Revelation

Charlie Becker
Being a Model

Look at us as art, archival bodies
already in black charcoal or brown ink
waiting to be drawn out, broad embodied
sketches and rust umber long poses, think
bring to life with texture, fine proportions
anatomy guides each line, the blending stub
cross-hatched skin, curled strands of hair apportioned
among shadows made by soft erased rubs.
Wise artists know we models are human
beauty, flawed perfect on canvas, paper
as they reimagine us and zoom in
fascinate all eyes with our savored
presence, sharing essence of a body
while being more than tangible bodies.

Ignatius Valentine Aloysius
A Miracle to Fight Anxiety's Covid-Raw Ataxia

The used Jetta wagon looked sleek and inky on
the dealership's website, butcher-like dicing all my
cannibal salivations with big price-tag, 38,000 miles,
and hidden horrors fleece-lining its pockets. I would
have to try it. So warm. Getting close, so hot.

Oh, and then I'd have to buy it, with instant
shameless financing. I felt that punch in my organs,
its servant, but recommended the car highly to the
roads and highways of Midwest America.

In return, the car elevated the wind and seasons
on my back, tied threads, broke bread on black matte
dash, and caught the spies of my innocence to
suspend their mining. This pregnant joy
set for myself only and not for others. Meanwhile,

The quiet strike of all its machined parts had
already begun before Covid, continued their quitting
ways in a private letter to my ignorance, which couldn't
name the offenders, officers, and subscribers to
the car's gradually suspending iron heart.

It broke its friendship with me. Made me a
prisoner of the rural lodge, took paper money and my
vote to hold on dearly to its steering wheel crush
and good storage. Gave me notice of its failing

With burst water pump, bad tie rods, rust-tight lug
nuts snapping off, power lines draining power
from a long-forfeited battery's pledge, heat sentries
killing-silly the AC, its rainforest floorboard on
the driver's side, sabered windshield wiper liquid line,
sunroof drips, and runaway leaks assuring the
general absence of air from tires living in disgrace
in front of my house.

And yet I bravely spared the sorry brow, showed
the world my honor, my promise to carry such
surprise through the false swells of luxury in such a
spiteful car. A new 1000-amp charger discharged
light and jump-power, raised my panic though

On days when streets trembled with advancing
patrols of trumpeting city trucks, pressing their weapons
against drugged and homeless leaves piled up in
tents all along curbside from end to end and
beyond. The city dished out its parking violations,

Tickets shot their volleys with perfect brutal accuracy,
no mercy, no miracle from Rome's regent in the
heavens, even as I prayed for exhibitions of strength
and medals. Then paid fines each time, so costly,
applauded my choice to stay away from the courts

And wring out the warfare of littleness from my
bones and ash, still demanding an eye for an
eye and the resignation of insults expunged from
under the car's cat-warming hood. Winter enforced

its own rules in Covid's death code, flung the
gates of alarm wide open. All my same silly plans
just died, crushing car in snow and dread shovel-pride,
so that it folded its arms and shook its head, then
went to bed like frogs and bears do, wired into
the season's frosting age.

*

The city came again in the thaw, with notices for
street cleaning and bull-horn-stapled law enforcers
in white branded cars, dressed with eyes flashing lights,
and their monster fights. I sprung Jetta again,
jumped my four-wheeled inky dagger and claw

Stalled in front by the big elm. Picked it up
from its chipped rims, and then drove it half a block
west to a T-bone corner on that busy side street,
a wounded road protesting the stampede from a
block south on Oakton. But Covid made life crawl.

As I brought the Jetta around, its engine cringed,
went silent and dark, hurled into its own trial orbit
without a spark or gait, while I sat in the balcony
of hope, behind a stiff wheel steering, my mask on,

Sat looking down at this immigrant life on stage.
I felt the murder of my moon deep inside the chest,

cold blood congealed as it flowed down
the beginning of April, none-too-soon, and I
took my feet outside, pressed

An earnest campaign at the skies of heroic blue
and savior light. *What should I do now?* I said,
waited for the souls of fourteen-thousand miners to
brave the tightest air in my throat and come
get me. The car locked its horns with the road at an
angle and aimed down against the curb, with
no palpable remedy. It cut off traffic in all three
directions, sent no blood supply to
those arteries. None--
What would you like me to do now? Cried again,

Endeavoring to tease a tow truck out of its Friday
pandemic contingencies. Stay with the corpse, abandon
nothing. Stay! Let the patron saint of drivers move this
plundering mountain through the raging crosses,

Through barbaric strain and skull. An inch will not do,
nor a year of it, just all, every measure of help that
heaven can provide. Then I heard the wheels, that

Ferocious animal roaring through dissected strength,
and I looked up over my left shoulder into
the yawning breath of impossible consequence.
In no place but there, where I stood then, came
a miracle to fight anxiety's Covid-raw ataxia. He

Stopped his landscaping pick-up truck behind me,
said *Do you need help? I'm Arturo.* I nodded.
He got out, put his Covid mask on as I pressed mine
against my face. In this warm current of benefit,
we were neither one nor the *other*. We became, at once,
all the inhabitants of these United States.

George L. Stein
momma francine and summer tacetta in tompkins square park

George L. Stein The Cineàste

George L. Stein take me to church – Xio and Momma Francine

George L. Stein when worlds collide

George L. Stein soft/hard – love queen layla

George L. Stein love

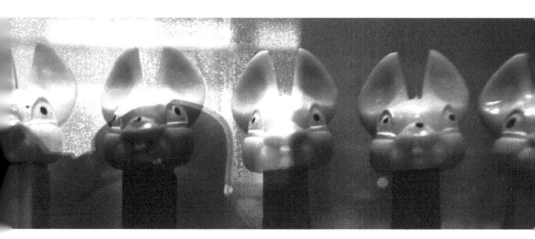

George L. Stein candy dispenser perp line-up

George L. Stein american dynasty

Holly Mathews
Whisperdrip

I thought I saw a clear-eyed doe tiptoe
duck around the gutter
that dripped all night

last spring loudly I didn't follow
no one would believe
me and I was balancing

an octopus mug of black
coffee on my knee
nursing my eternally

broken and lactose-intolerant
core organs or heart which I have long
doubted despite

the whisper of evidence
gathered now at the
chickadee feeder

I prefer to lay my trust
in the morning glory vine
which appears to be

rooted in truth
briefly angelically numinous
and impossible to remove

Holly Mathews
Stone Lion Parable

The boys set off in search of more lions, which was a thing in suburban New Jersey: stone lions guarding 4BR palaces of a certain class of striving whites. Someone should have told the suburbanites about rebar, or, I don't know, lion-glue, because apparently it had been a long time since the bland dads were adolescent boys with restless pulses rambling brains quick hands and urges. They hadn't imagined enough. But this particular night, ready with their paint and hammers and 4AM ideas, one boy said "Ready?" and the lion in question replied "Always" which naturally caused an uncommon pause so he went on "I once played panflute in macchu picchu, and a goddess rose from the rocks." The boys, still stunned, looked at each other. "Would you like to hear the song?" And one boy said "fuck no" so the lion tried another tack: "I agree completely with your heart," he said, which was nauseating of course, but true. The boys decided to light up, and the lion joined them with his pipe. "Every plant has roots, guys" he tried to say but saw they couldn't hear him, so instead of teaching them his brilliant endgame, he broke into a wild air-guitar solo and soon dawn rolled toward them over the GW bridge.

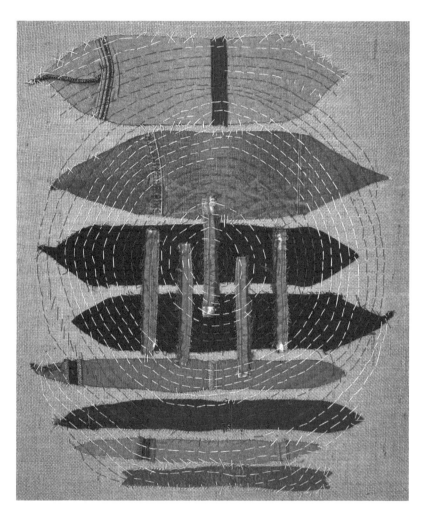

Kari Cassellius A Beautiful Gesture

Jones Irwin
I Became A Vernacular Dracula

Bloody Zoo that is society I swear
What Hegel was too cowardly to realise:
The animals in the big prison are only
The start of it. Their wardens pretend
To care for nature but what is nature?
A phantasm of virtue, a scourge of vice
That sweeps all weakened integrity before it.
We are all maggots. I remember the first night
I spent at Zamora prison where the worst inmates
Passed my teenage body around for fun. My love
Of the simple things was forever erased. Was
It any surprise then on that basis I became a
Vernacular Dracula?

Jones Irwin
Cookie and Max, aged 5

After a Nan Goldin photograph

There you are, little boy,

Art critic *extraordinaire*

And your Mummy

Will die soon of heroin

Leaving only – ART.

Jones Irwin
Empty Bed

After a Nan Goldin photograph

I have no need

To remember specific

Places or people

Those particular afternoons

Or early evenings

Which disappear

Ken Edward Rutkowski
On Behalf

The ground fire inside degrees stocks went higher and higher I walked through the brush across myself upon the stocks the green I flew no longer fell to the ground and briar the green never came through but the Brown discussed the Blower blew itself into my evil eyes they whispered to me of lies of things I knew they did not believe in the fires were Brown the green grass all around burned black the teeth that ground with souls they desire small people held in the grass all the people they kissed each other's ass pass assets mingle in chains that rattle in the Briars big desire big companies we're taking the human hand across the land and then chopping them off replacing them with wagons inside goats baaaaaa the most previous existence they say we want resistance we want to break free the results pulled me through the exam preoccupied tendencies the woman in the sea who called to me I did not resist I did not resist I held her and locked her up Called her by name inside the stocks were Brown the green grass all around the ground black down into the sound of the mare beating his hoof beats I did not hear a sound when the anger came I crossed the door across my arms afloat my chest I passed the stocks in through the best land of Golden sun that I once knew Brown and green down on drew the black hood of horrors and dust and the women we changed in the children remained all the people we blame black is dust the ground the grass the stocks built up taller than the small people the big ones they still kissed us we found someone we found someone new they sat in stone caskets in the wind in every new Gray built from the stocks they still grow around one tree left it sits by a ditch the best burn considered a circle around this earth black deep bewildered at birth the woman I change from the scene give birth to the baby that we love bless the kin this earth I'm sorry I apologize.

Ken Edward Rutkowski
Palm Wave

Palms take natural shape under water under a sign of relief from the hot sun they so dutifully protect me from I swim by under above sun yellow green dot in point in mind through water light down through the focus bright light blue in the stale shadow of my effort to remain still hot natural shape underwater under light with light but swim I must as the sun passes his reflection around down below the water the sound no more I hear no sound from afar of which we are not so sure we are all reliefs under the light the palms take natural flight shape underwater early from the sun the son of the hot protect me from my swing by above China watch the shadow watch the horn watch the baby being born in water by light go through the light green pinpoint night I see the middle of my eye come out like a big palm wave shout out my effort to remain still is not good enough but swim I must as a sound passes my reflection around it's around the sun goes up and down under the palm trees that ground no more sound water above the above we are leaves under the light of which we are not so sure.

Mario Loprete
FUCKOVID, Concrete Sculpture, 2021

Mario Loprete
B-boy 2015, Oil on Canvas, 100 cm x 100 cm, 2015

Mario Loprete
HARD CONCRETE, Concrete Sculpture, 2022

Mario Loprete
B-boy 2017, Oil and Cement on Canvas, 80 cm x 100 cm, 2017

Mario Loprete
B-boy 2019, Oil and Cement on Canvas, 100 cm x 100 cm, 2019

Mario Loprete
FUCK WAR, Concrete Sculpture, 2022

Liza Achilles
Sonnet 122

Your body's signage shows you're hankering
To talk with,—lay eyes on,—make love to me;—
But, patient and polite, you wait for green—
And only then the gas hit joyously.
The billboards of your soul announce in tall,
Prismatic letters that our traffic needs
To take it slow:—all crossroads at a crawl;—
Abruptly, though, you'll shift to higher speeds.
You say, since you're too scatterbrained to drive
Through multiple gals' signals, left and right,—
You'll zoom:—till you at love's red disk arrive.
Since I can't say who's—(yellowed you've my light)—
Hot-rodding toward your biz—with flashy eyes,—
Reluctantly, I'm chasing other guys.

Liza Achilles
Sonnet 123

What smell you in the glass, dear boy? I'm lost.
Tonight we meet again;—but, meanwhile, we've
Both dating profiles full of dregs we've crossed
Off of our lists,—while scheming we're to thieve
A winner from the competition's bar:—
A choicer one, that is, than you or me.
The used bookstore's, likewise, a reservoir
Of dull, picked-over pulp:—the matchless prix
Is in the new batch, just arrived!—and yet
Folks often overlook a dark horse wine,—
So I'll scan closely, taste and place my bet.
I'd rather blend my grapes with your bloodline!—
I think:—my taste buds can be hard to read.
My course?—I'll sip! . . . unless you intercede.

Liza Achilles
Sonnet 127

Sweet, handsome man:—this feels precarious!
While dating 'round, I'd think, if one's a dud—
(Lacks sex appeal—or ditches me)—no fuss
I'd make—but simply snatch a diff'rent stud.
More fraught is my relationship with you:—
I call you, 'gain, my boyfriend—ah, so nice—
My hard-won liberty, though, might unscrew,—
And how I'd suffer if you dumped me twice!
Last time around, you flipped when I spoke of
Fam'ly soirees,—so this time circumspect
I'm with all jeopardous discourse;—I love
You, though:—oh, this I longed to interject
Into our bedroom fusion! I held back;—
And now I'm tipping, gagged and maniac . . .

Lord Sterling
Kis Their Will, Angels Give It a Lick On The Cheek

The red ferrari kolour of her charlotte tilbury lipstick drives me above

limitations of speed that authorities with power enforce't

Adventurously I flow through the rhapsodic o highways of love

Befuddling all geographical intelligence with it's course

Let the top down feel the komplimentary air
The sweet coco mademoiselle parfum so fair
That it hypnotises the innocent roads
Making them dream of a celestial abode

With aspirational wing That scarlet Ibis romantically flies

past the golden magnificence of all vehicular bird

To choke in palpitations on it's smoke the noblest demise

Spoken from her emblazoned wheels in fiery word

O hand of the meadow open your palm wide
Veal the glamorous amaranth hidden inside
Along with the shining ignitional keys
Turn them balletically lets chase the breeze

The streets claimed that her walk is mean

But they never seen when she runs

Introducing luciferian chaos to a world serene

The El Diablo of rage here she komes

In the heat from the California sun on high
Across the rich Santa Monican pier we glide
Leaping into the obscure depths below
A melodramatical art gone..a lovely woe

Now we kruise thro an illicital heaven where only you and I xist

Ruffling the exquisite marabou fan plumes of a tempest

The Daytona and Nascar Seraphims chant ride fast as you wish

Here the law of automobilent sin is null and diminished

Melissa Cannon
Child's Kitchen

she's dreaming of baking something
something sweet and French

midnight snacks for her neighbors
the two women she saw
kissing with their tongues
deep in each other's mouths

she wasn't spying
they were right there out
in the open by their French doors

what can she bring them?
what gift? what offering?

when she wakes she's whispering
mes cheries   une petite corbeille
cherries soaking a crimped crust
pear tarts and custards

Leticia Priebe Rocha
í

My father forgot to add the accent in my name when he signed my birth certificate so instead of Letícia I became something in-between, muted and without a balance point, which

certainly helped when my family flew 8,000 miles and landed in a place where no mouth could bother to open wide enough for an í, where assimilation became the #1 lesson and my GPA never suffered, yet

it certainly didn't help when my house was possessed by bruises and screams, when this flimsy, í-less thing collapsed and could not stand up to him, could not unleash the í that would rupture the eardrums of everyone within 8,000 miles and save us all and now

I wonder if my father wished to go back in time when he got a call that his daughter had tried to "hurt" herself, if he wished he could add the í when he walked into the psych ward and saw this blubbery blubbering thing because

an í certainly would not allow herself to be infected by the need to die, yet it is this i that has survived in spite of its need to become an í.

Ellen White Rook
Two(mbly) by the Sea

~ I ~

Out there
     the words of my father
     expire
and sink

          What the sun left on waves after

               it sunk
            spun frippery

     Mask plaster stuck to their faces like bones or broken toys

Citrus
     or stone
   fruit
     lemon or more succulent
        Hello

       Is something out there?

Jealousy makes no waves
no logic but after dark steals deep

             Come to me

make a net of quiet
     and forgiveness

Islands and shores

          Children play too hard
     The wind
  cuts them
          into shovels and pails

Stories of rectangular rafts

      run aground

One captures the rest

Tides well

                                        Forensic

                                                 myth

unique

        fingers print

                                              Sadness without regret

                  grit and

    salt

        The illusion of stillness

Where   where   where

                    shadow

                        wood

                                              bone

~II~

You
cannot
erase every
trace
or the little
cries of big
birds
The poem
speaks to what is
not there
an object
with its
public
private attributes
words
trucked in bare
feet
exposed
to
clouds on a
golden
splendidness
The sea has
no one
looking
out down and across
An object has attributes
which we could call
fields
or qualities
The ease of
the sea is not
the sea
even
when the lines are azure
rough
and
clear

~III~

A poem to the sea is not the sea
The sea is a symbol of itself

It is not an eloquent reflection
or the tossing
of flotsam and jetsam
or moving
or muddying
or deep light
dark beyond treasure
or the myriad creatures

                                        Once upon
                                          a tide I
                                  invented mermaids
                                 and costumed little
                                              girls
                                 crochet seaweed hung
                               with star skeletons and
                                      scallop shells

A poem to the sea is at the edge
which is torn against a long silver rule that arcs
when you hold it like a sword
inviting advance

The paper tears wide open swaths
broadside shore to land on
when the tide is low

                                     Their tails were
                               iridescent pink and blue
                          They were my poems to the sea

It never disappears entirely
framed or rolled and tied
with a ribbon

                              They wore small crowns
                                they made themselves
                                   crumpling silver
                              foil around cardboard

Poem to the sea
has no code
to decode

There is no color intermediate
to green
and horizontal
to violet

They grew their dreams in slipper shells
hair bobbed and shone
on those days they floated
and were found
by sun

The poem is a symbol of itself
a gesture sand makes in an array
They do not exist without the other

Waves comb
sea snarls
the little mermaids dance
slipper shells
We write poems the sea
can read as it washes
even when
we are picked clean like
lead and chalk

The stain of the sea is not the sea
is not the poem of the sea
The sea reads
in its own rinse and rise
with epic ease

Karin Falcone Krieger
Diurnal Nature Journal Destroyed by Rainstorm: Images and Sonnets

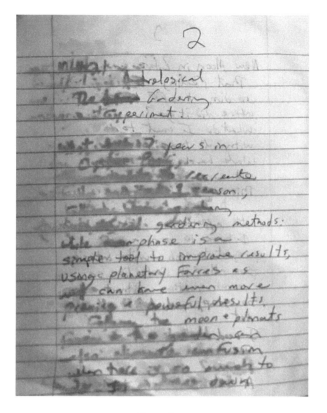

<u>Saturday</u>
To get manure from the best island, rescue a butterfly.
Go to places haunting sand, like the quiet of a fishing trip.
Movie tautog long to be loud, beside a pen.
Power is never as cool as the egg.
I dread the silence with bags.
Be something worse.
The bait is green, my son, the crabs.
They are so solid, so we are them.
Pages cut in half, to count on, alive.
I visit again, for our own decent food
I liked you, not factory farmed shit.
And it's sad, no social life this,
but exciting to fish.

<u>Commandments</u>

- Replace your papers with cannabis.

- Haul away the gathering moon.

- Sign the book of the Sisters of the Root.

- Pray to St. Crossroads for needles and strangled vines.

- Drink elixirs of the prying underground.

- Join the Thor Tour.

- Compost 'bout my island home.

- Free the vine you are of rail and land.

- Eradicate invasives on the particulars of astrology.

- Cut them into 3-foot lengths so the quick
  growing butterfly town homesteader can
  lasagna garden Noah's ark while Facebook
  loads.

- Cut another.

- Ready for apple butter adventure.

- Curb the almost helpful monarch when gardening.

- Burst into foliage in the spring.

I got it!

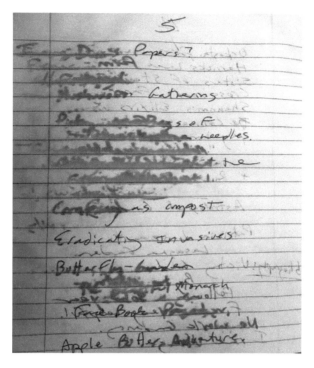

Landlord of Comet

Planting days by the bay at last!
Unwanted killing moon sign
in the cycle of work, significant.
I, landlord of comet
have covered the quarter.
All neighbors do keep
windows from Summer
and pull the fast that was left.
Plant growth was understood
but imported beetles and ivy attacked,
another interesting cure.
During a water sign's familiar import
I put to use the roots in water
which I want to see grow faster.

Mark Rosalbo Purple Surfboard

Uri Rosenshine
The Tea-Stall

In the newspaper
an avalanche has buried
twenty hikers
in the Himalayas.

A few survived, it says,
by taking cover
at a nearby tea-stall.

The word "residuum"
comes to mind, a chemist's word
but I don't mean it in that way.

Residuum, as if it meant
the destiny of things.

*

You need a scarf,
a good scarf for the winter months,

bags of salt, boxes of tea
and a snow shovel.

A scarf, like a zen koan
you can't remove, except

by meditation. Permanent knot
preserves the wanderer.

It gets colder, but you
are dressed in a sheep's costume.

Your sneakers break grass
on the frozen glade.

*

I come down from the mountains
The valley dims
I wander silently and am somewhat unhappy
And my sighs ask, Where?

A solemn code on the piano.
Then the wanderer, a baritone:
Ich komme vom gebirge her...
and I recognize his inflection

the voice of one
coming to an erasure
a blank place.

But the wanderer grapples with this:

Ich—
Ich—
Ich—

*

Why did we think it would be vacant here,
uniform?

It is dense and varied,
full of partial memories of final things.

The walk to work repeated,
the friends avoided,
the dinner conversation;
the wrestlers on the TV
in the evening.

Sometimes the quietness of things distracts us.
Then we fall again, through the inventory.

*

The umbrellas are open
drying in the hall.

In the window which once
seemed to convey seasons
the landscape has disappeared.

Where sparrows brawled
in the sand,
where grapevines hung
with blistered leaves,
where clouds dissolved—

immersion, fragmentation, disintegration, desiccation, dispersion…

*

Nothing is left
except the glass

which reflects
the room

the bed and the desk
yourself

facing a window
to an identical room,

the final identity
of your meditation:

Da ist

Nichts

Nichts

Nichts…

Vinicius Miranda
When People Make You Go Places

This new person,
even if just a prototype hardwired to reassure,
must have something better to say.
Then the old person. Who,
cross-wired and eying its broken nose the most,
can only blubber out the cartilage.

Revel in the think
of this new type of person. Of a heating system, blowing
smoke right up everyone else's chest and meaning it.
That furnace which crackles within,
with the piping that is crooked and lean,
bears a little breath. A whistle that scuttles across
the neck hair, just enough.
The warm mist builds up to a thick brume,
real good for opening up your pores.
Somewhere from which all of them tiny voices can slither out of.

Remember the smell of sea on the tongue.
Think: "And I don't know if we ever got to caring, like,
really caring at all." As you hug sand.
Love lives in the pit of the stomach
as an after-thought you comfort-ate.
In disgust you close your eyes. In the sun,
in the dark you see the shellfish chip pebbles with their claws, and
take platform shoes to the shoulders of a beached whale.
Leaving the home of a folded coral, crawlspace,
to study a mirror hung up off the bulging of a seashell.
It is wrinkled too.
Then they'd stuff sand up the scaffolding undersea,
fill up the cavernous with rough-round-the-edging.
Think: "Furnishings in the dark are just something to blow-up a toe through."
Someone else's kid comes up and
kicks your sandcastle down the embankment and
you open your eyes.
The thought-pollution in a jockstrap,
it gets to you.
It makes dirt out of anything.

Vinicius Miranda
Blue Nut

The fucks stain, our Tango,
when the carpet just chewed our rug.
Dancing the traumatic right through our wall.
And ceiling,
the fucks braid the minutes.
Latching onto our naked prosthesis, the tongue-tied into cornrows.
-

The Fucks lie between us,
spread-eagle on our upholstered drapery, off white, in rhinestone.
We hit our heads on the nightstand,
the night-sweats as varnish.
As Fucks spit on the back of your neck, on my ass-crack.
As Fucks crawl out of the belly of the mattress. Wearing memory foam, in
waist deep.
The Fucks find a hole, equal round,
caliber of your mouth. Veneer dentures at the cleaners,
in the creased underarm of our couch.
On the leftover backsplash tile. Soft cork out thumbed.
Then,
-

The *Fucks* palms us through the keyhole, onto the backyard,
takes over the house.
Every night, the *Fucks* prods our sockets.
The whole house dances flickers,
lights up like a Christmas faucet. Flooding
Tinker-bell feasting on a firefly.
Gorging on headlights.
Then,
 it fizzes darkness.
Champagne bubbles up and out the chimney,
all over our brand spanking new homelessness.

The ooze reeks of applause.

Joseph T.Y. Lee
Summer Impression, Oil on Canvas (digital)
3000 x 3000 pixels, Dec 2021

Zachary Dankert
Beaver Moon Prayer

What are you but a shaft
between winter skins pealing
bone to trachea
a farm dog's horizon howl

What do I see but genuflections
to the White River, cardinal directions
pointing down undertow throat

O moment of Flesh, mounting
between fleshless moments
red and wider than Lutheran oculus -
Rose Window - mandala

antlers of recluse trees
supping on my midnights heads
raised to ascension of heat.
Cornstalk wax, Heron wane,

dredgings of home parched
on bed sheets. When
I am anywhere else. House rubbed
in hand to be kept alive.

What do I see but a halo on
night -conquested roads shepherding
me to order's miscarridge

What are you but my suppliant breath
deprived of parallel mouth
thickening farmland's ink to words
then setting away to death

Zachary Dankert
Temple of

                                                  I

I'm not afraid
      of winding up   unoriginal
what scares me is my tongue
      grafted
      onto someone
            who turns back into this
                 sunrise
           blind from the heron's
               night-crowned shoulders
          it regards the world through a telescope (paradise)
Morning pools
      in aged September leaves
      that kill themselves   quietly
         before greenless, sink quietly
            through some future I may
         never ascend and return
          to the earth (sinkhole) around me   my scrying bowl
              unhelpfully
                showing the dull, dense monstrosity
                    of my younger self
     out of this pit
         the sky   a shattered iris
            a hungry ocean   a maw
        this woman I hallucinate
         before I wake, she responds
         in a beat out of tune
           with a world (body)
         hallowed   excavated
           of opal bones
              a house (a commonwealth)
          where one light is always flickering,
              a clock always ticking
           to an end past jesus
            bereft of it's North Star

II

I've robbed myself of something
        not in my poems or
        the vacuum between bodies (passages)
a red berry drops from the honeysuckle
hands depart the other's heartbeat
           afterthought;
                fireflies fortune-tell before a lightning storm.
On my chest
        a stone containing my mother's heart
        and my father's heart, containing
           a ruptured vessel watering
           oak vigils of our house
I'm not scared
        of men
        but of my outline, in midday sun
           chalk marking
                archaeology
                      of a corpse
I didn't want to be
        found I only
        wanted a matriarch
           like this dark, old one
        crucified to hold
           my temple of suffering
           and whisper a blackbird's departing
                strain, a rosary
                white-fronted geese carve
                    around the planet.

III

Sunset disguises distances
        this world (personhood) is so much closer to itself
in this, I understand; I've lost
        something under Indiana farm fields
                        evening compressed together into
                                sedimentary organs.
        This stumble to the peak
                only permanent as a child's
                                oxygen before being
                        sold to a question.
        What's that in your eye? Another continent
                drifting by
                a humpback whale dream (intangible gardens)
                        In this great Arctic Circle
                                of years,
                                moon dark and ice muted
                where we wave at
                        monoliths scarred
        with our suppositions.

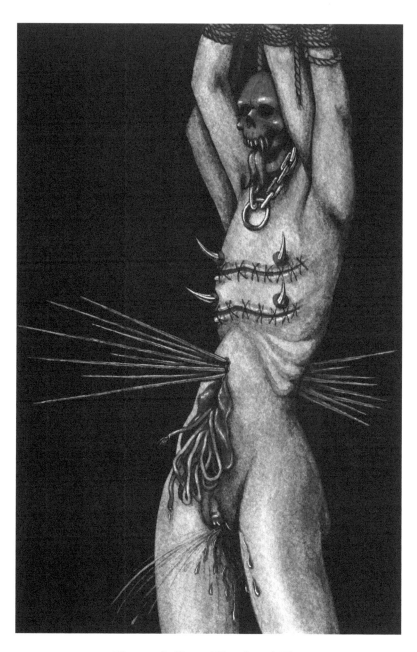

Kenneth Zenz Blood and Piss

Dualtagh Mcdonnell Late Waiting

Dualtagh Mcdonnell
What I Do While I'm Waiting

I have decided that
I'm going to make you a rug,
and it feels like saying it all
and never doing it,
filling the empty space
with the things that used to be on the walls
filling up with talk, coffee, mornings?
filling up the space with everything we know.

Talking to the wall and telling it
that I'm afraid of cows now
and I just need you to know
- they're aggressive,
I can no longer leave my house
without a car.

The cows come and you walk
and that's all you need to know,
standing there at the end of your road,
talking and waiting.

What I should have told you
was that I always thought about
what it would be like if we were neighbours,
but now you're asking to be my friend
and I don't quite know how that works.

Standing there and talking,
not to fill a silence
but to think of what it would be like
if someone was standing next to you,
to keep those words and hold.
Holding.
Something to contain it all,
these things and your strings
hanging in the trees
with your feet framed at the bottom.

Pink love caught taut in this wool
and pictures of you.
I think it works better if I
don't know what you think right now,
that you wait and I deliver this
quiet and discreet.

Edward Thomas-Herrera
Fine dining chez Minotaur

My mother could not wait for me to stop nursing so she could push me off her lap and get an unobstructed view of her more attractive children. I tried to prove my worth. I learned to juggle. I perfected the art of the double entendre. I developed a really good eye for pulling nits out of hair. But take one lousy bite from one lousy arm on one lousy palace guard - suddenly, everyone's hiding behind the tapestries, cowering in fear. They built a labyrinth for me to play in, a sandbox that combined astronomical possibility with zero hope. I know what it's like to feel

abandoned. I've been there. I'm still there.

I feel sorry for these coltish young boys with their strong backs and their clear skin and their poor sense of direction. These flower-soft girls, firm breasted, firm buttocked, hymens intact, choking on their saliva, dripping with sweat: they have my sympathy. I take no pleasure in watching them soil their special occasion garments. To think that those loins could have spawned entire generations of philosophers and statesmen! All that potential for wielding a scythe or a hammer or a shuttle or learning to juggle: wasted, shameful, sad.

But what, pray tell, have the Powers-That-Chef prepared for my table this year? Same thing as always: hearty peasant stock, the cream of Athens. It's not that I particularly enjoy eating human flesh. It's that human flesh is the only thing ever on the menu. Given half the chance, I'd most eagerly consume an unripe fig, an unpeeled fava bean, an apple core, an olive pit. I'm guilty of a tragic weakness for grains - if it grows on a stalk, consider it comestible. I believe in a balanced diet. Nutrition is very important to me. Not that anyone's ever bothered to ask. Food is life. I only draw the line at beef.

I like to engage my fellow wanderers in feather-light chit-chat. I ask them their names. I ask them their ages. Show interest in their hobbies. Crack a raunchy joke. It serves to break the ice. I lead them on a guided tour of the place. Here, a choice spot for napping. Here, my favorite corner for thinking about, you know, the universe and stuff. Here, the ceiling is high enough for juggling practice; I always say it's important to keep one's skills up. Here, nothing to see. Here, nothing to see. Here, pardon my mess. Here, a dead end where I keep all my junk - every home has one. Here, you don't want to know. Trust me.

Sometimes, we strike up a rapport, the kids and me. One can sense the temperature of the room cooling from extremely panicked to not-so-extremely-panicked. Most welcome. It alleviates the lonely. It's a break from my usual masturbation routine. If we must crawl ever forward toward our inescapable graves, it helps to pass the time with a quick game of tag or maybe hide-and- seek. I'd offer my guests a little something to eat, but I'm afraid all I ever have on hand are leftovers and I've got a hunch that they wouldn't be very much interested.

But compassion has its limits. As does patience. And I, unsurprisingly, hardly qualify for sainthood. Especially when my stomach starts to growl. What choice do I have then but to continue participating in a system of oppression masquerading as civic duty that relies on a plentiful and expendable underclass? It's not personal, mind you. It's just dinner.

Edward Thomas-Herrera
The fall of Troy, night desk clerk at the Ramada Inn Lodge, Santa Fe, New Mexico

My forebears painted their faces with boar's blood, braved Baltic waters, split enemy skulls wide open with double headed axes, sang their praises to gods of fire and thunder and skiing. The German lady staying in Room 240 is demanding to know why smoking isn't allowed in the hot tub.

Before responding, I stroke my ginger beard, allowing a be-ringed hand to linger upon the painted beads I braid into my facial hair whenever management isn't looking. I draw strength from their wooden provenance. I bought them off this Norwegian guy I met at Burning Man. He told me they were carved from an ancient oak growing just outside of Bergen. Seemed legit. I think his name was Einar.

The phone rings. An electronic room key refuses to cooperate. The phone rings again. A luggage trolley has gone mysteriously missing, last seen in the vicinity of a blonde family from Ohio. No one ever calls to wish me a pleasant eventide or a good morrow. No one ever stops by the front desk just to compliment the runic tattoo inside my wrist which reads "strength" or "might" or something like that. I don't speak rune.

My way is that of a lonely warrior. A lonely warrior for hire. Like a samurai, only the night desk clerk version of the Viking version of a samurai, whatever that is. That would make a cool graphic novel if you ask me. A lusty tale of defending tribal territories, composing sagas, drinking copious amounts of mead, and making vigorous love to many, many grateful large- breasted women. Blonde families from Ohio seem to be under the impression that luggage trolleys just magically return to their owners, like the mighty Thor's mighty Mjölnir. Tom Hardy could play me in the movie version.

The phone rings. The free Wi-fi password refuses to cooperate. The phone rings again. A clogged shower drain. New guests arrive. Can you direct me to the nearest Starbucks? What's the best way to avoid altitude sickness? Can you tell me the difference between New Mexican cuisine and just regular Mexican? Heavenly Father Odin, I pray you deliver me from these tiresome tourists in search of turquoise squash blossom necklaces and paintings of howling coyotes, silhouetted by the full moon! In Valhalla, a hero's place awaits me at the banquet table. In Valhalla, we have no need of shower gel.

The German lady staying in Room 240 brandishes an unlit Marlboro in my direction, defiant Teutonic countenance mauve as a turnip. Such is my Ragnarök. Bereft of sword or spear, I parry with the only weapons at my disposal: a blank stare, a heavy sigh, a leaden monotone. Cigarettes are only permitted in designated smoking areas, Ma'am. Fear me.

Edward Thomas-Herrera

The knife that killed Johnny Stompanato on the evening of April 4th, 1958

I've always considered myself to be a utensil of exceedingly modest ambitions. Although I've been known to open the occasional parcel tied with string, I was fashioned to recognize the tendons that held a chicken together, or the way strips of fat curve on a pork chop. Once, I was enlisted to unclog a garbage disposal (not my idea). That was a mistake.

I've always considered my universe to be a simple, compact affair: tile countertops and stainless steel sinks, the hum of a Frigidaire. There was the ever-present scent of scouring powder, of bloodied, pink butcher paper, of that fraught, noxious moment when gas escapes the stove top right before it meets with a lit match.

I wasn't looking for any trouble. Honest. I was just lying there, like I do every night, in my usual spot, clean as an unread newspaper, taking up space in a cutlery drawer lined with oilcloth. I harbored no dark, ulterior motives, no grand design. My only aim ever has been to serve.

Yes, I heard shouting. Yes, the slamming doors. They were impossible to miss. I recall the sound of the girl's breath, approaching from a distance, fast and heavy. I recall the loud, plastic snap of a light switch, her footsteps making the rounds of the kitchen perimeter, the hand that took hold of me and forever re-named both our futures.

You know, she wasn't entirely to blame. A primordial instinct convinced her some problems are best resolved with the threat of violence. Fear pointed me in his direction. Luck landed me between his ribs. Panic pushed me through his skin. Anatomy and geometry did the rest, throwing a torso full of vital organs into my trajectory.

Now I'm reduced to artifact, tagged and photographed, sealed in a manila envelope, filed away in some dusty box on some dusty shelf in some dusty corner of some dusty evidence room. Now no one cares if rust sets in or my blade grows dull. Now my useful days are behind me.

Perhaps it's all for the best. Pain and surprise have always been an occupational hazard, but only as far as clumsy cooks were concerned. Sever a man's aorta, you become a token of poor judgement and nobody wants to see you cubing a slab of chuck for Sunday night stew anymore.

Gabby Gillam
This I Know

The soil of upstate New York
is nourished with my ancestors
bone and sinew broken down
persisting in roots and branches.

That I shed blood and tissue
to create a copy of myself
incubated him in a public library
fed him books and songs so he sings
Hamilton to his graphic novels.

This fleshy husk is finite
HydrogenCarbonOxygenNitrogen
a kindness the universe lends us
that will return to soil and stardust.

Gabby Gillam
Worry Stone

When my edges are worn
smooth and you can press me

like a worry stone between
forefinger and thumb to calm

your mind, I'll know how water
can tumble you until the cracks

and grit are scoured away—leaving
a shine that's soft but unbreakable.

Gabby Gillam
Raised Catholic

The roots of your faith were buried
deep—hidden beneath stubble
and calloused skin as you shifted

weight from foot to foot
back pressed against the wall

—a piece of flesh on your tongue
and then straight to the car.

The hymns didn't hum in your chest.
The prayers rarely crossed your lips
but you held up that wall every Sunday

and I wonder if the altar boys recited
the routine of your memory

if every congregation
of sin smells the same

if you confessed while waiting
in the parking lot—found
absolution in the open air.

Shelly Rose
Bonanza

Am I doomed to wander this prairie
The same prairie where my great great great grandmother
broke her back
where God or someone or other saved her
and taught her to walk again
no pull the wagon my family lays claim to
Am I doomed to pull that same wagon
until its wheels splinter my spine into
 a million tiny pieces
as numerous as the grains of sand in this lovely Deseret

Can my love only be found in casinos
lurking behind cameras and strutting around slot machines
never honest and always wanting
the elaborate carpet the same as my living room
the illusion of endless night, and no clocks on the wall
growing smaller and smaller until the paint's chipped
and the bullhead threatens to crash down
onto the car my mother borrowed three days ago
to more or less die in the Bonanza
Am I doomed to pull that same wagon.
Will the Bonanza be waiting for me
when the lake's all dried up
the bullhead hanging
by a single wavering thread

Lissa Batista
Portrait of My Mother American

I've tried to keep betta fish twice. Their beauty in the blue prisms of their scales, gulping air
from the water's surface, no longer dependent on their gills. Territorial little fucks, they thrive alone, their tails like mermaid's hair flicking in the wind, a femme fatale's exit in an action movie. My mother has hair like that.

My mother is a crown tail betta, in a fish tank— all eyes, sleeping, floating, hiding under the
kelp-colored blankets.

My mother was born on a farm, playing inside a cow's carcass. She describes this memory to me
in naive bliss-- cow's blood, hot. Ribs malleable, fencing in. A cow dies, my mother goes outside. She learns to cleave out its organs, holding the lungs in both hands. Fat with tissue. Ballooning.

For days, the betta ride slime bubbles of algae flowering from sedimentary food flakes between
neon rocks.

My mother loved watching *Carrie* in the 80s because she was always the prom scene— always
covered in blood, wanting to get out of the small town.

Both times I cared for Bettas, I left them with my mother. She bought them a hammock, a
floating, plastic leaf. My mother, on her handwoven hammock in her bedroom.

My mother became American through the hands of my father. He switches her Havaiana sandals
to sneakers with socks, her legs for a bike and a bus pass, her knife for cleaning supplies, her cows for pots and pans. Find my mother in the kitchen or with Andy. Her hands rip open pillow sheets to stitch back into a ghost costume for Halloween. Her hands no longer carve, they create.

I find my mother hammocks herself in a memory of carcassed cows, she's wrapped up in
kelp-color blankets in bed, the Bettas lost their mermaid hair, she's lost all her knives.

When Bettas get sick, white spots appear on their body, the water intoxicates them, the sludge
makes it harder for them to swim in, their fins, paper-thin, weakening. They shed their tail, they float, gulping air from the surface. They are resilient, but they know to give up.

Lissa Batista
I Tarot You

Let's sleep on a twin bed— face me, hold me into
a staring contest, I don't care who wins but I'm counting
on your toothy-open-mouth laughter, your pink uvula

hammocked between tonsils waking up, legs like vines
spiraling until afternoon, don't brush your teeth
let's kiss with tongues, eyes open, smother our noses,

can you guess which taste
bud loves you most.

I want to hear about the secrets you don't tell your best
friends, cry until the pillow sponges, pinkypromise,
kiss our hand, spit in our palm, swear you won't

tell your next wife, although I've pulled your tarot cards,
the Lovers Card came up twice— the bodies open palmed,
chained engulfed in fire conversation with the devil

Let me just say who cares,
The Lovers are at peace—

they wake up without caring of bad breath, the farts under
the covers, the toe wrestling, the crease of the cotton pillow
horizon on their cheeks, belly up, arms like vines, open palmed.

Lissa Batista
My Darkness is a Dare

I want to lay out our crystals under moonlight and bathe in reflections as we talk about ghosts
in forms of haunted homes, of our past. My darkness is the moon,

for as much darkness covers my existence, there is a lightness that surfaces in cycles, in the way I let you lightyear through my secrets, show you my tarot deck, pick a card and play a rom-com.

How close can I get to you with language wrapped around our tongues before you give up
a kiss on the cheek for familiarity, a kiss on the corners of my lips, on the lips

on purpose, on the scuros of my neck for falling into playing with me. My darkness is a lake,
you raft to see what it takes to engulf me in gallons— how long will it take to realize as you telescope your way through my limbs, there are parts of me missing in craters

full of things I refuse to share? — how sex is a defense mechanism, that I want you to finger
my thoughts with National Geographic facts about red foxes who burrow in each other's faces to remember each other's scent before going hunting.

Lindsey Bottino
Crumble

& soon after she leaves,
you'll discover that your house
doesn't stand without her.
That somewhere between the headaches she gave you
and the affection she showered you with,
she became the foundation—
on which you rest your feet.

You're a tile piece,
and she's the whole goddamned floor.

Njord Njordson Apple

Njord Njordson Alterations Plinth

Marcella Simon Eyes of Wonder

Marcella Simon Letting Go

Phoenix Kai
My Wilted Home

I am rooted at my door. for I fear
rejection behind my plumage.
imagine, I invite you in my home.
your eyes widen at the damage.
languidly, you inspect the room.
charcoal, bitter in your nose.
you peel back the carpet
exposing secrets. hidden floorboards.
luggage in the deepest recesses.

I cannot restore scars to my home,
so I watch from a window
a sunny day.
enclosed four baring walls
steeped in solitude.

dream an empty hole.
junk protrudes. from a chest,
my shame. violently visible
to a mere stranger who didn't bother
to remove boots after entering.

telltale weight breathes and groans.
clawing outward. calling
salvation and I ask
you. plug your ears
as I have done.

Paul Lobo Portuges
bullets curse barrio poets…

bullets

curse   who

barrio   eat   then

poets   them   spit

             like   out

             dulces   histories

                        of

                        pain

Andrew Demcak
In the Rehab, I Am Given Plath's *Ariel*
  for Sylvia Plath

Yours was a suicidal line, well read.

You wrote out of crisp bones, ankles, and fine wrists.

Nooses of tendon, your stringencies.

We'd have gotten on like a room in flames.

What mattered but bloodletting?

It produced poetry by the armful,

unloosing pages of sonnets from glands.

Had you sensed letters forming words in your veins,

their great need to be translated,

while I slice my bookmark along your page?

Andrew Demcak
A Birthday Present, Three Days Sober
 for Anne Sexton

What to do with these borrowed bones if they are too sick or
small?

Feel your elbows at their ugly edges.

Skulls have a surplus of fragile spots.

Don't be embarrassed like curtains which don't possess a
window.

The ghosts won't mind your annunciation.

The ones writing up the rules, those select measurements.

Be bedded gladly in flesh, the invisible ways.

The breath dragged out, some ancient beast from its secret
lair.

Your gelatinous pastiche.

After all, you are impermanent.

Your body that the elements admire, then eat.

Andrew Demcak
Waking in Winter, Rehab #3

Dead clianthus in pots like hairy skulls.

December elms have become iced gloves.

Winter's tin, crisp taste dulling the night air.

The itch and buckle of immobile groves.

I cultivate an orchid that asserts itself out of season.

Its buds come on like brandy.

Flowers are rhetorical.

Nerves immolate themselves.

Petals unfurl impossible tones of August resorts.

Gordon Blitz
Hockney

92 million record for a living artist
California pools bubble up
Smoky mountain terrain
Visible smog
Shadow swim dropping
To the cemented blue bottom
Blonde hair ruffled
Orange sports coat defies age
Breathe in the chilled air
Pierce the blank
Stare at the dead body
Flapping drowned in thought
Green money trees
Printing my living room

Gordon Blitz
5.3 miles to LACMA

Exploring fantasies and fairy tales
Franz von Stuck's 1911 lithograph
Eyes me
Corneas stares at the unshaven face
Healing my sore feet
Restoring the leg muscles
Warming the chilled eye brows
Dashing through the exhibit
The remedy for loneliness
Packing in the curative therapy
Willing myself to return
Public transport solves aching limbs
The tap card paves the way
Fairfax dips into Santa Monica
Splendid transfer timing
I ask if I need to tap charge again
Annoyed Bus driver says yes
As I sit, she anoints me
Hey, you with the hat
Her call beckons me
Free transfers within two hours
Lady Driver makes a happy ending
For my fantasy fairy tale.

Gordon Blitz
Free Moca on Thursday

Soaking in Manny Farber and Termite Art
Itchy boys with their art girlfriends
Rothko waiting in the wings
I'm coming apart at the seams
Obsessing without relief
Lunch circulating in my throat
Turkey meatloaf salivating my mouth
Dream of a snail pace
Rehearse happiness
Practice my fingernail falling off
Stop hiccupping memory blips
Document the sparkling chandelier
Big bang silver lights
Hammering the installation
Chat the docent
Did you meet the artist?
No, but I heard he's nice
Coming from away will hold me tonight

Aaron Hoge Imaginary Landscape

Aaron Hoge Wood-Man

Aaron Hoge
When the collars were long

When the collars were long,
Towering brown Sasquatch jumped out of my KISS lunchbox, "old buster"
"You are mighty cute."

When the collars were long,
Rode the Quassy Lake Carousel sea monster,
Green, whirring, winged, horse-head, mermaid-tail, Kindergarten zoology
chocolate, reddish brown, Okapi, *Loved that slender giraffe face,*
White horizontal striped legs.
Dangerous adult penny arcade silver KISS pinball machine, "Shock Me," Ace
Frehley, my teenage hero,
Tilt awhirl carny blasting ZZ Top, "Got Me Under Pressure," Styx 8-track,
Grand Illusion, red corvette, *wicked awesome!* When the collars were long.

When the collars were long,
Energy blade Sunsword slashing Thundarr was my hero,
Leonine bad-tempered Ookla clubbing the bad guys, *supersonic excellent!* "Angels
on the Balcony," soothed me,
"Like a fire burning in a stone."
When the collars were long.

When the collars were long,
Cast spells like Gandalf, lived in Middle-earth,
Stole rubies, emeralds, gold from Tiamat,
Pilfered musty Playboys from an abandoned house down the street, Hid them
in a stone wall, read them on the sly,

When the collars were long.

When the collars were long,
I was a white crane style pecking, flapping monk, in love with Bruce Lee,
Coveted a *wicked* gold Italian horn necklace I saw dangling from the neck of a
dude, "Half penny, two penny, gold Krugerrand," JY, another secret hero,
"Eddie now don't you run,"
But I ran, ran, ran, like bionic Steve Austin on the green, past the enormous
white gazebo, Rainbow Nike emerald green Duncan Butterfly Yo-Yo pot of
gold, &
Flew, flew, flew, like Hawkman over Harrybrooke Park & red Lover's Leap
Bridge, When the collars were long.

Lord, three black whippets sat under a birch tree, When the collars were long.

Brian L. Jacobs
HOMOCAUST HOMOCAUST

Sati pyre phakelos yomiagne yells
in all the light we cannot see

gather thee faggots
and fly up wing'd achene's unsolfege'd fire bush

exiled in stuprum's botany
at birth's dirge

I face the faggots I gathered
numb as angels' rejection deployed

a blue print here
for disintegrates

Allen Ginsberg
up in flames

corpse me
poetic

dragged into Reagan death pits
where James Baldwin is Martin Luther Queen's comic eunuch

and where he and Walt Whitman
marry testicles in hand

Chico Starr Untitled I

Chico Starr Untitled II

Chico Starr Untitled III

CONTRIBUTORS

Liza Achilles is a writer/editor in the Washington, DC, area. She is published in Beltway Poetry Quarterly, the Washington Independent Review of Books, and the Silent Book Club blog. The focus of her blog (lizaachilles.com) is seeking wisdom through books and elsewhere.

Ignatius Valentine Aloysius earned his MFA in Creative Writing from Northwestern University, where he won the distinguished thesis award for fiction. He teaches as an adjunct lecturer at Northwestern's Weinberg College of Arts and Sciences and in the Writing Program at the School of the Art Institute of Chicago (SAIC). Ignatius is the author of the literary novel Fishhead. Republic of Want (Tortoise Books, Chicago), and his writing has appeared in Third Coast Review, TriQuarterly, The Rumpus, Newcity, The Extraordinary Project, among others. He was a 2020-21 Creative Writing Fellow for the Ludington Writers Board and the Ludington Area Center for the Arts in Michigan. Ignatius is co-curator of the popular reading series, Sunday Salon Chicago. He also sits on the curatorial and diversity boards at Ragdale Foundation in Lake Forest, Illinois. @ignatius2u / www.ignatiusaloysius.com

Abol Bahadori has actively shown his work in the UK, Washington DC, Maryland, and Virginia. His first major solo show was in PEPCO Edison Place Gallery in DC with more than 85 paintings on display (2011), later in Aron Gallery, DC (2012) and DESI Gallery Arlington, VA (2013). His works are regularly selected and awarded by the Art League Gallery, Alexandria, VA, with a solo show in 2021. He also routinely been juried in for Washington DC's most anticipated art event; The Washington Project for Arts (WPA) Auction Gala. He has worked in various creative fields throughout his career. As a fabric designer, graphic designer, art director, and currently creative consultant, he's solely relied on fine arts and his continuous painting process as a source of inspiration. As well as a foundation for his professional life, painting is also his livelihood. He considers himself more of a colorist. For Abol color is everything. Color comes before shape and form. It creates space, dimension, and—most importantly—feelings.

Lissa Batista is a Brazilian-born poet raised in Miami, Florida where she is an MFA candidate at Florida International University. Between teaching middle schoolers and mothering her preschooler son, her favorite time of day is snack time.

Charlie Becker is a retired speech pathologist who now studies and writes poetry with the Community Literature Initiative in Los Angeles. He also has helped bring poetry to under-served high school students through the Living Writers Series and L.A. Unified School District. Charlie's first book of poetry and drawings, Friends My Poems Gave Me, was published by World Stage Press in 2016. He has also had poems published by Passager Journal, Comstock Review, The Dandelion Review, and Silver Pinion. Charlie lives with his partner, Aubry, in Laguna Woods, California.

Gordon Blitz as a child was called a sissy, girlie, fag, queer, and homo. Getting towel whipped, stomach punched and spit on were part of his world. His father, who died after Gordon's Bar Mitzvah, berated him with shouts of "Walk straight." Gordon never found his writer's voice until he retired in 2017 from forty years of accounting and became a passionate writing machine. During 2020, Gordon had published work in Whoa Nelly Press, Wingless Dreamer, Two Hawks Quarterly, the Santa Monica College Journals Chronicles and On Going Moments, and Gay Wicked Ways. In 2021 his best-selling novel "Shipped Off" was published and is also available as an audiobook. On February 2022, his second novel "Fathers and Other Strangers" was published. Ten of his autobiographical stories are available on the Queer Slam Episode 21, podcast called "Just Gordon." Gordon has been a member of the oldest LGBTQ synagogue in the world Beth Chayim Chadishim since 1990.

Lindsey Bottino recently received her MAT and teaching certificate from Sacred Heart University. She is now a middle school ELA teacher. She has previously been published in the book Paradise Poetry, the literary magazine, "In Parentheses" and literary blog, "sadgirlsclub." When she is not reading or writing, you will find her painting.

Melissa Cannon lives and writes in Nashville. She is an old (nearly 76), cranky(!), queer (in all senses of the word) poet who has had careers in academia and in fast-food. She writes in a variety of forms--from experimental to formal--and on a wide range of topics--from queerness to the occult. Her work has appeared in many small-press journals and anthologies over the years, including ABLE MUSE, BITTER OLEANDER, IMPOSSIBLE ARCHETYPE, INDEFINITE SPACE, KENYON REVIEW, PLOUGHSHARES, SINISTER WISDOM and SLANT. She was the winner of the inaugural Willie Morris Award for Southern Poetry.

Kari Cassellius lives in Hollywood, CA where she works as a costume tailor. She often reverts to a feral mode of being where she just wants to make stuff and the rest of the world is but an annoying imposition.

Zachary Dankert is a recent graduate of Hope College, where he studied Biology and English. His poetry can be found in South Florida Poetry Review and Wingless Dreamer, and is forthcoming in Breakbread Magazine, Peculiar, and The Fourth River.

Andrew Demcak is an award-winning American poet and novelist, the author of six poetry collections and eight Young Adult novels. His books have been featured by The American Library Association, The Lambda Literary Foundation, The Best American Poetry, Verse Daily, and Kirkus Reviews.

Gabby Gilliam lives in the DC metro area. Her poetry has most recently appeared in Tofu Ink, The Ekphrastic Review, Cauldron Anthology, Instant Noodles, MacQueen's Quinterly, and three anthologies from Mythos Poets Society. You can find her online at gabbygilliam.squarespace.com or on Facebook at www.facebook.com/GabbyGilliamAuthor.

Karin Falcone Krieger lives and writes on Long Island, New York. Her poetics, essays, opinion, and journalism appear in BlazeVOX, Contingent Magazine, The Laurel Review, The Literary Review, Able Newspaper, Newsday and other publications. She holds an MFA from The Jack Kerouac School of Disembodied Poetics at Naropa University in Boulder, Colorado. She taught freshman composition from 1999-2019 as an adjunct instructor at several area colleges. Her gardening and other projects can be seen at karinfalconekrieger.com

Edward Thomas-Herrera is a Salvadoran-American native of Houston, Texas, currently residing in Chicago, Illinois. He graduated from Rice University with a bachelor's degree in musicology before studying directing at the Theatre School, DePaul University. Since leaving drama school, he has become a fixture of Chicago's solo performance scene. He was a long-time artistic associate with Live Bait Theatrical Company from 1991 to 2008 and a regular contributor to THE ENCYCLOPEDIA SHOW from 2010 to 2012. He is also one of the co-founders of BoyGirlBoyGirl, an ensemble of solo theatre performers which mounted over a dozen shows from 2004 to 2016. Edward is the author of five plays (OF DIAMONDS AND DIPLOMATS, MONDO EDWARDO, THE PARAGRAPH, THE BRITISH EXIT, and DRESSING FOR BATTLE), two solo shows (COCKTAIL CONFIDENTIAL and FUN WHILE IT LASTED: A FAREWELL TOUR), and one as-of-yet-to-be-produced musical (HELL IS FOR THE VERY HOT). Currently, he is hard at work on a new script entitled OPPORTUNISTIC CHORUS GIRLS OF 1934.

Aaron Hoge is a visual artist and a writer. With over 40 years of art-making and multiple performances and exhibitions, Aaron is a seasoned professional artist. Using the mediums of drawing, painting, performance, video, writing, and photography Aaron's work explores intersections between loneliness, becoming, homosocial relationships, and futurity. Drawing inspiration from a wide range of sources such as cave paintings, graffiti, Expressionism, Imagism, Vorticism, English Literature, Western Esotericism, and Philosophy, his studio practice represents an abiding interest in language, text, choreography, semantics, poetry, and the creation of striking visual images. Aaron becomes what he is through his visual art and writing. His lifework is the integration of all aspects of the human personality.

Jones Irwin teaches Philosophy and Education in Dublin, Republic of Ireland. His vision is of a postmodern existentialist, with a dash of noir mixed in with a progressivist ethic. He has been featured before in Tofu Ink.

Brian L. Jacobs is a poet and editor of Tofu Ink Arts Press. Brian grew up in Southern California and has been teaching GATE English and Humanities for twenty-nine years in both K-12 and college settings. He lives in Pasadena and has been married for 16 years to Thye, a Professor of Nursing and a Nurse Practitioner. Both Thye and Brian are currently working on their PhD's. Brian was the assistant to the Poet's Allen Ginsberg and Julie Patton, during his time at world while on a peace pilgrimage with Buddhist monks commemorating WWII visiting Europe, the Middle East and India. Brian is also a three time Fulbright Scholar, which has allowed him to study in Brazil, where he studied its water issues; China, where he studied its vast 10,000 year history; and Japan, spending time to participate in a case study in one of its small towns near the Japanese Alps. He had also earned a National Endowment of Humanities grant to China, studying its philosophies and histories, a Fund For Teachers grant visiting South Africa, Swaziland and Lesotho, plus earning other various grants that have taken him to places all over in the United States. He also taught teachers at a university in Fuzhou, China for five summers under grants from SABEH. Subsequently he has earned an Earthwatch grant to the rainforest of Ecuador, to study climate change and caterpillars and he recently earned another Earthwatch Senior Fellow Grant to teach teachers in Acadia, Maine studying climate change and crabs. Brian has been to 110 countries and had visited all 50 states, practices Yoga and is a proud vegan. Brian's poetry has been published in several publications including, Shiela-Na-Gig, the Crank, The South Florida Florida Poetry Journal, Progenitor Art and Literary Journal, GRIFFEL, Foxtail, Rip Rap, The Bangalore Review, Sunspot Lit, Anthropod, Pa'Lante, Dark Moon Lilith Press, Black Tape Press, Genre, Inky Blue/Celery, Red Dancefloor Press, Entelechy, 1844 Pine Street, Pasta Poetics, Trouble and Praxis. Brian marinates in inspiration from Gilles Deleuze, Richard Rorty, Audre Lorde, Edouard Glissant, Reza Abdoh, Marlon Riggs, Tim Miller, John Fleck, Karen Finley, Essex Hemphill, Patricia Smith, James Baldwin, Walt Whitman, Pedro Almodovar, Keith Haring, NEA Four, Justin Phillip Reed, The Beats, Paul Celan, Artist Nick Cave, Sam Rami, Jean Rhys, Erasure, House Music, Robert Duncan, The Smiths, Lee Edelman, John Waters, Lana Del Rey, Patti Smith, Michel Foucault, American Visionary Arts Museum, Kurt Vonnegut, ACT UP, Daniel Day Lewis, Radiohead, PJ Harvey, Lady Gaga, Zhang Huan, Arthur Danto, Derek Jarman, Kiki Smith, Marc

Almond, Nina Hagen, Grace Jones, This Mortal Coil, Boy George, Bjork, Divine, Tracey Thorn, and Florence Welch.

Phoenix Kai (they/she) is a queer poet, writer, and multi-media artist based in Seattle, Washington. Their work is forthcoming or published in Beyond Words, Sweet: A Literary Confection, and elsewhere.

Joseph T.Y. Lee has more than ten years of experiences in branding, marketing and retail communications. He lives in both Singapore and Malaysia. In 2019, he started his own agency, JLTY Atelier, which specialises in brand and product development. From 2010 to 2013, he volunteered at Project X, a human rights organisation based in Singapore that provides social support and health services to people in the sex industry. A linguistic graduate and polyglot, he speaks English, Mandarin, Malay and French. He has passion for the arts and travel, and occasionally, paints & writes poetry.

Mario Loprete I live in a world that I shape at my liking. I do this through virtual, pictorial, and sculptural movements, transferring my experiences and photographing reality through my mind's filters. I have refined this process through years of research and experimentation.
Painting for me is my first love. An important, pure love. Creating a painting, starting from the spasmodic research of a concept with which I want to transmit my message this is the foundation of painting for me. The sculpture is my lover, my artistic betrayal to the painting that voluptuous and sensual lover that inspires different emotions which strike prohibited chords.
This new series of concrete sculptures has been giving me more personal and professional satisfaction recently. How was it born? It was the result of an important investigation of my own work. I was looking for that special something I felt was missing.Looking back at my work over the past ten years, I understood that there was a certain semantic and semiotic logic "spoken" by my images, but the right support to valorize their message was not there.
The reinforced cement, the concrete, was created two thousand years ago by the Romans. It tells a millennia-old story, one full of amphitheaters, bridges and roads that have conquered the ancient and modern world. Now, concrete is a synonym of modernity. Everywhere you go, you find a concrete wall: there's the modern man in there. From Sydney to Vancouver, Oslo to Pretoria, this reinforced cement is present, and it is this presence which supports writers and enables them to express themselves.
The artistic question was an obvious one for me: if man brought art on the streets in order to make it accessible to everyone, why not bring the urban to galleries and museums? With respect to my painting process, when a painting has completely dried off, I brush it with a particular substance that not only manages to unite every color and shade, but also gives my artwork the shininess and lucidity of a poster (like the ones we've all had hanging on our walls).

For my concrete sculptures, I use my personal clothing. Through my artistic process in which I use plaster, resin and cement, I transform these articles of clothing into artworks to hang. The intended effect is that my DNA and my memory remain inside the concrete, so that the person who looks at these sculptures is transformed into a type of postmodern archeologist, studying my work as urban artefacts.

I like to think that those who look at my sculptures created in 2020 will be able to perceive the anguish, the vulnerability, the fear that each of us has felt in front of a planetary problem that was covid 19... under a layer of cement there are my clothes with which I lived this nefarious period.

Clothes that survived covid 19, very similar to what survived after the 2,000-year-old catastrophic eruption of Pompeii, capable of recounting man's inability to face the tragedy of broken lives and destroyed economies.

Holly M. Matthews is a poet and mental health social worker with bad knees and a zumba habit. She lives with her family and pup in Portland, Oregon. She credits her pandemic survival to zoom poetry workshops facilitated by Christopher Luna.

Dualtagh McDonnell lives in Dublin where he studies English and Drama Studies at Trinity College Dublin. He has recent works published in Jelly Bucket Magazine and High Shelf Press. You can find him @dualtagh_.

Vinicius Miranda is a Brazilian born French-Canadian, currently writing out of South-Florida. His written work has been, and/or is to be, featured in issues of Coastlines Literary Magazine, The Dillydoun Review, and a Crack the Spine anthology. @doarc.vinicius

Njord Njordson was born 1972 in Arlington Virginia. Now lives in Reston Virginia.

Paul Lobo Portugés teaches creative writing at UCSB, taught at UC Berkeley, USC. Books include Falling Short (2020), Sorrow and Hope, Breaking Bread, Hands Across the Earth, The Flower Vendor, Paper Song, Aztec Birth, The Body Electric.

Leticia Priebe Rocha received her bachelor's from Tufts University, where she was awarded the Academy of American Poets University & College Poetry Prize. Born in São Paulo, Brazil, she immigrated to Miami at the age of 9 and currently resides in the Greater Boston area. Her passion for writing emerged as poetry became the only way she could untangle her experiences with mental illness alongside her intersectional, politicized, and stigmatized identities. Her poems are a reflection of the never-linear path of struggle, healing, and the search for home. Her work has been published in the Tufts Observer, the Awakenings Review, Rattle, and elsewhere.

Ellen White Rook is a poet and teacher of contemplative arts residing in upstate New York and southern Maine. She offers workshops on ikebana, Japanese flower arranging, and leads Sit, Walk, Write retreats that merge meditation, movement, and writing. Ellen is a recent graduate from the Master of Fine Arts program at Lindenwood University. Her work has been published in Montana Mouthful, New Verse News, Red Rock Review, and Trolley Literary Journal. In 2021, two of her poems were nominated for the Pushcart Prize.

Mark Rosalbo was raised in Leeds, Maine. He spent much of his early childhood exploring along the banks of the Androscoggin and Dead Rivers, the latter one of only a handful of rivers in the world that can flow in either direction. Early life socio-economic hardships shaped much of Mark's artistic choices as a composer, actor and painter. Many in his circle, including his brother, succumbed to various cancers like Leukemia as a result of living along Maine's rivers once polluted by paper mills. After graduating from high school, Mark moved to Los Angeles to study at The American Academy of Dramatic Arts. After graduating from AADA, he moved to NYC. He also became a successful trader on Wall St. and remained in the city until shortly after 9/11 when he moved his family to Vermont to enjoy the banks of (this time much cleaner) rivers.

Shelly Rose is a musician, Far Side comic reciter, and sweetheart of the pines. She enjoys knitting, gardening, and sitting very still. She lives and dies by the grace of the desert, and she doesn't know how she wrote anything, it just happened by accident. She has two cats, one of which is named Tomb Raider. She is currently working on her second album for her project Yucky Bangs.

Uri Rosenshine lives in New Haven, Connecticut, where he works at a wine store. His poetry has appeared in the Missouri Review, Right Hand Pointing, and "Minutiae: Three Poems," a chapbook published in collaboration with Directangle Press.

Ken Edward Rutkowski lives in southern Vietnam. His work has appeared in Tofu Ink Arts Press, The Fiction Pool, Synchronized Chaos, Fiction International (Fall 2021), The Journal of Experimental Fiction, Paragraph Line and Borders: An Anthology of Whatcom County Writers. While in Asia, he has traveled around Vietnam, Cambodia, Indonesia, Taiwan, Malaysia, Borneo, the Philippines and Sri Lanka.

Marcella Peralta Simon is a retired Latinx grandmother, splitting her time between Cambridge, UK and Kissimmee, Florida. She has been a diplomat, university professor, and instructional designer. She writes poetry and short fiction. Her artwork has been published in Smoky Blue Literary and Arts Magazine, Beyond Words Literary Magazine, Persimmon Tree, and The Acentos Review. Marcella explores her Latin American roots and background in political activism to create passionate commentary on the tribulation and joy of the human condition.

Chico Starr (Amaris Sanden) is a musician and has been doing art since age 5, and is currently 22 years old. He is very excited to work with Tofu Ink for his second time to spread his message that creativity is something that everyone possesses.

George L. Stein is a photographer living in the Garden State and endlessly working on his portfolio. He works in the art, street, urban and rural decay, alt/portrait, fetish, and surreal genres. georgelstein.com

Lord Sterling has been writing poetry based from multiple prophecies he received at church 17 years ago. His dream is to make a living from writing. As he worked in the hospital throughout the pandemic I was inspired even more to take advantage of the time that I have left on the earth.

Kenneth Zenz is a Chicago based artist who illustrates from the perspective of an ill trans masculine body. He explores how gender, body modification, disability, technology, mental health and identity embody themselves.

CPSIA information can be obtained
at www.ICGtesting.com
Printed in the USA
LVHW070623210622
721686LV00001B/2